CONTENTS

Help in a crisis   6
Born on a battlefield   8
A special mission   12
Structure of the Red Cross   16
Conflicts and their aftermath   18
Emergency action   24
Working with others   30
Closer to home   33
Looking to the future   37
How you can help   42
Glossary and further reading   44
Index   46

Help in a crisis

A young African soldier, no more than fourteen years old, injured and bleeding, is carried into a large canvas tent where other wounded patients are being treated.

While the wind whistles around them, two women pull a Pakistani boy carefully from the ruins of a library. The boy is unconscious, and the women place him gently on a stretcher and wrap him in blankets.

Teenagers in a British shopping mall watch first-aid instructions on an interactive whiteboard. They compete to answer questions in an on-screen quiz, before trying out rescue techniques on a life-size dummy.

A convoy of Red Cross trucks heads for Kigali in Rwanda, where civil war broke out in 1994. The Red Cross is one of the first international organizations to arrive at the scene of a crisis.

The International Red Cross

Sean Connolly

W
FRANKLIN WATTS
LONDON•SYDNEY

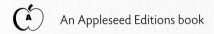
An Appleseed Editions book

First published in 2008 by Franklin Watts
338 Euston Road, London NW1 3BH

Franklin Watts Australia
Hachette Children's Books
Level 17/207 Kent St, Sydney, NSW 2000

© 2008 Appleseed Editions

Created by Appleseed Editions Ltd,
Well House, Friars Hill, Guestling,
East Sussex TN35 4ET

Designed by Helen James
Edited by Mary-Jane Wilkins
Picture research by Su Alexander

ISBN 978 07496 8071 8

Dewey Classification: 361.7'634

A CIP catalogue for this book is available from the British Library.

Photograph acknowledgements
page 6 Patrick Robert/Sygma/Corbis; 8 Stapleton Collection/Corbis;
10 C.I.C.R.Vernier Jean Bern/Corbis; 11 Hulton-Deutsch Collection/Corbis;
13 Corbis; 14 Vernier Jean Bernard/Corbis Sygma; 16 C.I.C.R.Vernier Jean Bern/
Corbis Sygma; 18 Corbis; 20 CICR/Kokic, Marko/RCRC National Society;
21 Gyori Antoine/Corbis Sygma; 23 CICR/Bigler, Roland/RCRC National Society;
25 Olav A. Saltbones/International Federation; 27 Charles W Luzier/Reuters/
Corbis; 29 Guatemalan Red Cross; 30 CICR/Stoessel, Marcel/RCRC National
Society; 31 Colin Chaperon/American Red Cross; 32 Mark Snelling/British Red
Cross; 35 Jon Jones/Sygma/Corbis; 36 Layton Thompson/British Red Cross;
37 Yoshi Shimizu/International Federation; 38 Phil Vine/International Federation;
41 CICR/Heger, Boris/RCRC National Society; 42 Bernd Thissen/DPA/Corbis
Front cover CICR/Stoessel,Marcel/RCRC National Society

Printed in Hong Kong

Franklin Watts is a division of Hachette Children's Books

These scenes remind us that the world still has many people who are willing to help others – giving up their time, maybe some earnings and even their lives. Each of these scenes is linked to a single international organization – the International Red Cross and Red Crescent Movement, sometimes called simply the Red Cross.

Many members – one movement

The Red Cross helps people in emergencies, or helps them learn how to prepare for, or prevent, such emergencies. Much of its work is linked to medical aid, in keeping with its birth on European battlefields nearly 150 years ago.

Today the Red Cross movement is a wide-ranging international organization. But unlike organizations in which orders go to local branches from a central headquarters, the Red Cross does much of its work 'from the bottom up'. At its core is a group of 186 national Red Cross societies. These societies are the lifeblood of the movement, as they are the first contact people have with the Red Cross in times of crisis. The societies work together with the two other main elements of the Red Cross movement, which concentrate on warfare and natural disasters. The examples above highlight these three roles.

The seven core values

The International Red Cross and Red Crescent Movement operates wherever it is needed. It is often the first international organization on the scene in a crisis, and the last to leave. All Red Cross activities are guided by the movement's seven core values. These help the movement shape and direct services and programmes all around the world.

The seven core values are:
• humanity
• impartiality
• neutrality
• independence
• voluntary service
• unity
• universality

Born on a battlefield

The Red Cross movement was born in the middle of the nineteenth century at a time of great change and progress in the world. Unfortunately, not all this progress benefitted humanity.

New railways and telegraph lines connected distant parts of the world. But these inventions and others like them also made it easier to wage war on a grand scale. Generals could send thousands of soldiers – and powerful weapons – to battlefields with ease. Instant communications meant that military information could be passed on swiftly, opening

The British nursing pioneer Florence Nightingale, shown here in an Istanbul hospital, introduced new standards of hygiene during the Crimean War. Her contribution came less than a decade before the founding of the Red Cross.

the way for more intensive fighting. Europe was at the forefront of these developments, and suffered from their negative consequences. European countries were among the most advanced in the world, but its soldiers had more power to kill and injure than any before.

Some people, such as Florence Nightingale in the Crimean War, began to improve conditions for their wounded soldiers. But there was no international organization which would help wounded soldiers on both sides of a conflict.

Birth of the Red Cross

The Red Cross was to become just such a movement. It came about because a Swiss businessman followed a French political leader to the scene of a bloody battle. Henry Dunant met Emperor Napoleon III of France at Solferino in 1859 on a business mission (see page 10). The deaths and injuries he saw there affected him deeply.

Dunant wrote about what he had seen in a book called *A Memory of Solferino*. This book was published in 1862 and described the battle in vivid terms. More importantly, it called for relief societies to be set up in different countries to care for wounded soldiers and civilians. In addition, Dunant wanted a wider organization to give these relief societies a sense of purpose and shared aims. Those representing such an organization could display an emblem which would show their neutrality and keep them safe on the battlefield.

In 1863, a group of five men (including Dunant) organized a conference in Geneva to set Dunant's plans in motion. Sixteen countries sent representatives to the conference. The representatives decided that a red cross on a white background (the reverse of the Swiss flag) would be an ideal emblem. They urged governments to support and recognize Red Cross relief societies in their own countries. In effect, this 1863 meeting was the founding of the Red Cross movement. More accurately, it was the first meeting of the International Committee of the Red Cross.

From riches to rags

Jean-Henri (or Henry) Dunant was born in 1828 in the Swiss city of Geneva. He came from a wealthy, religious family. His father was a leading businessman who believed in helping others who were less fortunate. Henry held similar social values when he began his own business career.

During the late 1850s, Dunant set up a company in Algeria (then controlled by France). The company desperately needed water to operate, and Dunant had to apply for special permission to pump water in. He decided to approach the leader of France, Emperor Napoleon III, directly. The emperor was leading troops at Solferino, helping the Italians to overthrow Austrian rule. Dunant arrived in the middle of a terrible battle. The violence and confusion of the battle – and the inadequate medical help for the wounded afterwards – affected him deeply.

Over the next few years, Dunant concentrated on improving conditions for those affected by war. We know that his efforts led to the founding of the International Red Cross in 1863. During the following decade, he contributed to other humanitarian efforts, but his business failed. He was never given permission to use water in Algeria. This failure made it hard for him to face people at home in Geneva.

Dunant slipped quietly from public view and for more than 20 years lived almost like a beggar. He was recognized when living in the Swiss village of Heiden in the 1890s, and the world rushed to honour the man who had done so much for others. Despite these honours – including the first Nobel Peace Prize in 1901 – he remained in Heiden for the rest of his life. He gave his prize money to charities and asked to be buried in the simplest grave in Heiden. This last wish was granted when he died in 1910.

'Would it not be possible, in time of peace and quiet, to form relief societies for the purpose of having care given to the wounded in wartime by zealous, devoted and thoroughly qualified volunteers?'

Henry Dunant, A Memory of Solferino *(1862)*

Nearly 30,000 soldiers died or were wounded during the Battle of Solferino, which lasted for more than nine hours on 24 June 1859.

A special mission

The Red Cross movement had begun

when people's power to kill and injure had increased
dramatically. During the year of its birth in 1863,
the United States was torn apart in a brutal civil war.
This war was the first in which machine guns, iron-
protected ships and submarines were used.

During the civil war thousands of Americans died, suffered terrible
wounds or were held as prisoners of war in appalling conditions.
People in other countries could see the future of war as they read
reports of the events in America.

Rules of conflict

In 1864, when the Red Cross committee was just a year old, it urged
the Swiss government to invite representatives of other countries
to a conference. The aim of the conference was to find a way of
preserving some form of humanity during warfare. Fifteen European

countries attended, as well as the US. At the end of the conference 12 countries signed an agreement which became known as the Geneva Convention. Many other countries signed up to it later. The Geneva Convention called for a set of actions agreed by both sides in a conflict. These amounted to rules of war. At the heart of the convention was the need to treat medical teams helping wounded soldiers as neutral and to protect them as far as possible from danger. Warring countries today still pay attention to the Geneva Convention.

The Great War

The Red Cross movement could impose some rules on the way wars were waged, but it could not prevent wars happening. This became clear in August 1914, when Europe became engulfed in a terrible war. Called the Great War at the time (and the First World War now), this four-year conflict involved battles in many parts of the world. More new weapons – including tanks, poison gas and fighting aircraft – appeared during this war.

Red Cross nurses take babies to the safety of a sandbag shelter in Panne, Belgium, during the First World War.

By the time the war ended, more than nine million soldiers had died. Throughout the war, new Red Cross national societies were formed because of the appalling bloodshed and loss of life. In 1919, the League of Red Cross Societies (now called the International Federation of Red Cross and Red Crescent Societies) was formed.

New symbols – same message

Despite its Christian symbol, the Red Cross has never wanted to be thought of as a religious organization. It did not want people to think that its cross was intended to convert other people to Christianity. The symbol was chosen to represent the centuries-old tradition of sanctuary that Europeans found in churches. The new organization wanted to keep this idea of neutrality (not taking sides) in the battlefield. The symbol was also a version of the Swiss flag (which has a white cross on a red background); Switzerland is known for its neutrality.

The movement has welcomed other symbols which suggest neutrality. The Ottoman Empire, which was Muslim, chose the Muslim crescent rather than the Christian cross in 1876. The Red Crescent has remained the symbol for Islamic countries ever since. A third major symbol – the Red Crystal – was accepted in January 2007 for countries that choose not to be linked to either Christian or Muslim traditions.

Two familiar emblems – the Red Cross and the Red Crescent in front of the Red Cross headquarters in Geneva.

The work of the Red Cross no longer began and ended on the battlefield. A new Red Cross element aimed 'to strengthen and unite, for health activities, already-existing Red Cross societies and to promote the creation of new societies'.

Paying for the Red Cross

The International Red Cross movement spends hundreds of millions of pounds each year in carrying out its work. The three main elements of the movement (see page 17) use different methods to raise funds, although the donations are voluntary for each of them.

The International Committee of the Red Cross (ICRC) spends more than £410 million every year. This money comes from governments, national Red Cross societies, international organizations such as the European Union and donations from private companies and individuals. National Red Cross societies also rely on voluntary donations.

Some, such as the American Red Cross and British Red Cross, raise many millions through a wide range of methods (see pages 34–35). Red Cross national societies in poorer countries can raise only a tiny fraction of these millions.

The gap between the richest and poorest countries is reflected in the budget of the International Federation of Red Cross and Red Crescent Societies. The federation relies on the national societies for its income, and it uses a formula to decide how much each society should contribute. Richer countries must take on a larger share of the federation budget.

WHAT DO YOU THINK?

Footing the bill

The International Red Cross is constantly looking for new ways of raising money. Would it be better if the movement gave up the separate hunt for money and came under the umbrella of another organization such as the United Nations? Or does receiving money from many different sources give the organization independence because it does not rely too greatly on any single donor?

Structure of the Red Cross

Although people often use the
name International Red Cross, the organization's
official name is the International Red Cross and
Red Crescent Movement.

The movement is made up of three different strands, which deal with
warfare, development and disasters around the world (see panel). This
structure allows each part to concentrate on one place or activity.

International conferences

The most important decisions about the movement are taken at
international conferences, usually held every four years. Each of the
three main elements in the Red Cross movement sends representatives.

*The letters CICR, the French
abbreviation for International
Committee of the Red Cross,
sit below the flag which
flies on top of the Red Cross
headquarters in Geneva.*

Three elements

The three elements each have a special role.

International Committee of the Red Cross (ICRC)

The oldest element continues to look after those affected by war and other conflict. It remains neutral, directing and co-ordinating aid for the victims of warfare. The ICRC is based in Geneva and has offices in more than 80 countries, with about 12,000 full-time employees. It is made up of three governing bodies: the assembly, the assembly council and the directorate.

National Red Cross and Red Crescent Societies

Each of the 186 national societies helps the government of its country with health and development issues, disaster relief and – in times of conflict – care and treatment of the wounded. The societies raise money for their own operations and to help fund the federation.

International Federation of Red Cross and Red Crescent Societies

Like the ICRC, this branch operates around the world. It concentrates on helping the victims of natural disasters, rather than those caught up in fighting. It also helps national societies work together, both in disaster relief and in planning ahead. Federation decisions are taken by its secretary-general, who is elected at the federation general assembly (held every two years).

Together they work out new goals and ways of achieving them. A council of delegates (also with representatives from each element) meets every two years, helping to shape conference goals.

The standing commission makes sure that the aims and decisions of the conference are put in place in the years between conferences. This commission is made up of nine members: two chosen by the ICRC, two by the federation and five by the conference itself.

WHAT DO YOU THINK?

Too complicated?

Do you think the Red Cross organization has too many separate elements? Might it run more smoothly if all its elements (development, health, disasters and war) were brought under one umbrella?

Conflicts and their aftermath

A Red Cross ambulance meets a wounded Japanese prisoner of war in Hawaii as he comes off a transport plane at the end of the Second World War.

The Red Cross movement came into being because of the terrible fighting during the nineteenth century (see pages 8–11). Fighting and warfare remain an ugly feature of life in the twenty-first century, and the Red Cross continues to play a vital role.

The branch of the movement devoted to conflict-related relief is the International Committee of the Red Cross (ICRC). ICRC medical teams, volunteers and hospitals operate in the middle of some of the worst scenes of conflict. They are at the forefront of medical aid and are a visible presence even as bombs rain down nearby or speech is drowned out by constant gunfire.

... ON THE SCENE ... ON THE SCENE ... ON THE SCENE ...

African nightmare

Neva Gigliuk is a Canadian nurse who was part of an ICRC team which worked in Rwanda during 1994. At the time, this small African country was being torn apart by a civil war. The centre of the worst fighting often changed unexpectedly, keeping everyone on edge.

'The location of our hospital had been notified to both sides of the fighting forces. We had a ten-foot Red Cross flag identifying our position. And the people inside were under the protection of the ICRC. The anxiety level increased incredibly as we could hear the fighting approaching us.' Eventually soldiers from one side arrived.

The 32 wounded patients in the hospital were their enemy. 'Sheer panic set in! These soldiers were terrified that they would be killed... Three hours later the opposing military commander visited us at the hospital. We explained our position – that no arms existed within the hospital and that the staff and patients, including the wounded military, were under the protection of the Red Cross. The wounded soldiers needed the protection given prisoners of war (POWs).'

Despite the fierce fighting going on outside, the commander respected the Red Cross medical team and allowed the hospital – and its enemy patients – to move to a safer location away from the fighting.

The rules of war

Apart from the important job of providing medical aid in areas of fighting, the ICRC promotes international humanitarian law (IHL). This set of guidelines, sometimes called the Geneva Convention, tries to protect those who are involved in fighting, as well as civilians who are caught up in a conflict. The guidelines promoted by IHL are sometimes called the rules of war.

It might seem odd to expect people who are trying to kill each other to obey sets of rules. But remember that a war is like an argument between individuals, except that it involves more people and has far

Taking on cluster bombs

Some of the most important work of the Red Cross takes place away from the battlefield. The International Committee of the Red Cross (ICRC) uses its strength and reputation to fight for changes at the highest level. One of its biggest concerns is the use of cluster bombs in warfare. Since November 2006, it has pressed the United Nations to ban these weapons.

Cluster bombs contain dozens or even hundreds of smaller bombs that separate from the main bomb. These smaller bombs – sometimes called bomblets – usually have small parachutes. These are caught by the wind and spread across a wide area such as an airfield or a military base.

The Red Cross concern is about what happens next. About 40 per cent of the smaller bombs – each the size of a can of fizzy drink – do not explode immediately. After the fighting stops, they become a lethal risk for local children, who are attracted to the bright colours and parachutes. There are huge numbers of these bombs. In Lebanon alone, some experts believe that there are still 1.5 million unexploded bomblets which were dropped during the fighting in August 2006.

Red Cross officials monitor the tense ceasefire in Sarajevo, the Bosnian capital, in 1994.

Opposite page
A Red Cross inspector, identified by his sleeveless tunic, examines a damaged block of flats in Lebanon in September 2006. More than a thousand Lebanese died in the fierce fighting between Israeli and Hezbollah forces.

more serious consequences. Sometimes, two people who are arguing do or say something that makes it hard for either side to back down. Armed conflict is similar: if one side or the other acts cruelly, then the opposing side will find it hard to work for a peaceful solution. Its soldiers will be tempted to look for revenge.

The International Red Cross Movement has developed seven fundamental principles to make IHL easier to achieve and preserve. Broadly speaking, they are:
• People who are not directly involved in a conflict should be protected from harm by all sides in a conflict.
• It is forbidden to kill or injure an enemy who surrenders or who is not involved directly in the fighting.
• The wounded and sick are under the care and protection of the side that controls them. The emblem of the Red Cross, Red Crescent or Red Crystal should be displayed in areas where these people are kept or treated – to add to their protection.

Rebuilding a country

Isabel Gutterres is secretary-general of the Timor-Leste Red Cross Society, one of the most recent national societies to join the International Federation of Red Cross and Red Crescent Societies. Timor-Leste, formerly East Timor, is a tiny island country in Asia. It was a Portuguese colony for centuries, and neighbouring Indonesia took control when the Portuguese left in 1975.

As a student, Gutterres joined the struggle for independence against Indonesia, taking part in many protests. Life became dangerous for the protesters, and she had to leave her country in 1986. She returned in 1999 when the country became independent.

By that time Gutterres had completed her training as a nurse in Australia. Since then, she has worked to rebuild her country, helping its Red Cross national society become accepted in the wider Red Cross movement in 2005 (it now has 10,000 members). For her, the Red Cross can do more than simply make sure that local people have good medical care.

'The Timor-Leste Red Cross Society has an important role to play in helping heal the wounds of the unrest, through its activities, its volunteers and the seven fundamental principles. I have always worked with people. Now it's also about helping my country. To me, nothing could be more important.'

• Captured soldiers and civilians should be treated humanely. They should not be punished and should be allowed to contact their families and to receive supplies from outside.

• No one should face cruel punishment or torture. No one should be held responsible for an action they did not commit.

• All sides in a conflict should limit the weapons they use. They should not use weapons that cause unnecessary suffering.

• All sides in a conflict should distinguish between civilians and those involved in fighting. Civilians and their property should not be targeted by either side.

*Opposite page
The Timor-Leste Red Cross Society has played an important part in rebuilding the war-torn island since the Timorese gained their independence in 1999.*

Cuban captives

Since 2002, the United States has imprisoned suspected terrorists in sections of its naval base at Guantanamo, on the Caribbean island of Cuba. The ICRC has sent teams to inspect the prison, and has criticized the United States for the harsh conditions. The ICRC argues that it is wrong to hold people for months without charging them with a crime. Do you think the Red Cross is right to get involved, or is it hindering efforts to fight terrorism?

WHAT
DO YOU
THINK?

Emergency action

A terrible noise and shaking woke the residents of Yogyakarta, a city on the Indonesian island of Java, at dawn on 27 May 2006. Buildings toppled and caught fire, cracks opened in roads, and cars were tossed about and crushed. The city and its surrounding region had been hit by a strong earthquake, which measured 6.3 on the Richter Scale.

More than three million people live in Yogyakarta and the surrounding districts. The earthquake was centred on one of these districts, Bantul, where 80 per cent of the buildings, including a hospital, were destroyed. Dazed people wandered through Bantul, looking for families and friends who were still trapped in the rubble.

Thousands of people had died in the first few minutes. Afterwards more than 200,000 people found themselves without food and shelter. Even water supplies had been damaged by the earthquake.

The race was on to save others from death. The survivors needed immediate medical aid.

Springing into action

The Red Cross response showed its teamwork and effectiveness at every level. The PMI (an abbreviation of the Indonesian Red Cross) had 400 staff and volunteers on the scene within hours. They provided emergency medical aid and helped to plan long-term relief. Later that day, the IFRC launched a £5.6 million appeal. As the scale of the problem became clearer, the appeal target was raised to £16.7 million.

The PMI (Indonesian Red Cross) were quick to act in May 2006 after a devastating earthquake tore through the heart of the city of Yogyakarta.

This response is typical of the Red Cross when faced with a natural disaster or emergency. The IFRC is the organization that governments and the media turn to when they need information about a crisis. It provides information thanks to its thousands of members (linked to national societies) who constantly check the situation at the site.

As well as providing information to governments and the outside world, the Red Cross itself benefits from these contacts. The IFRC can publicize changes to its strategy in the crisis; just as importantly, it has a chance to press for more money to deal with the crisis.

Cross-border cooperation

Natural disasters do not recognize national boundaries. Storms, droughts and earthquakes can affect whole regions, involving many different countries. The Red Cross needs to react efficiently in such cases, ensuring that the national societies in the affected countries have enough help, that they in turn can help each other and that the rest of the world has the latest information about urgent needs.

Opposite page
Powerful and destructive hurricanes such as Katrina hit some of America's southern states each summer. The American Red Cross mobilizes special disaster relief vans to take food and emergency supplies to people, even before rebuilding begins.

Emergency response units

Within days of the Java earthquake, the IFRC mobilized three emergency response units (ERUs) to help with the relief operation. ERUs are made up of teams of specialists and pre-packed sets of equipment ready for immediate use in disaster zones. Each ERU had a specific aim:
• A combined US-Spanish ERU focused on basic relief equipment.
• The Danish ERU helped with communications (phone lines and mobile phone communications had been knocked out by the earthquake).

• The British ERU concentrated on logistics, making sure that people and equipment could be flown into the region.
Arnulv Torbjornsen, head of IFRC operations in Indonesia, explained how this fast approach was made possible by the way the Red Cross is set up: 'ERUs are an excellent example of how the movement uses its unique network of national societies to respond to crises immediately and effectively. The units boost the capacity of the Indonesian Red Cross to respond to local needs.'

... ON THE SCENE ... ON THE SCENE ... ON THE SCENE ...

Coping with Katrina

Hurricane Katrina, which destroyed much of New Orleans in August 2005, was the biggest test of the American Red Cross in its 125-year history. More than 1300 people died in the disaster, which also caused damage estimated at more than £43 billion. Bob Howard was part of the team which coordinated the American Red Cross relief effort.

The Red Cross provided almost a million free meals a day to hurricane victims. It gave shelter to 450,000 people. The total bill for food and shelter came to £185 million. In addition, the organization provided victims with £780 million directly, to help them recover their lives. Howard recalls that some people criticized the Red Cross efforts, saying that they were too little and too late. This view is wrong, he says, arising because the Red Cross was involved in so much:

'We have had sporadic criticism, but when you are the most visible you are the biggest target,' Howard said. 'To put it into perspective, what other organization could muster and galvanize 225,000 volunteers over a two-month period? Because of our structure and capacity we have been able to bring to bear almost a quarter of a million volunteers – a Herculean response.'

Hurricane Mitch, which struck Central America in October 1998, was an example. This was the most powerful storm ever recorded in North or South America, raking the region with destructive winds and dumping more than 2000 mm of rain. Thousands of people died in floods and landslides, and from disease as a result of the hurricane.

The Red Cross response helped the region get back on its feet. The four national societies (in Honduras, Nicaragua, Guatemala and El Salvador) made their needs clear to the IFRC, which sent supplies and experts. It mounted international appeals for aid, raising the amounts requested as it became clear how bad things were. Some national societies in other parts of the world sent workers and equipment to help in the recovery programme.

Opposite page
Mexican Red Cross volunteers prepare sacks of food for emergency aid after Hurricane Stan hit their country in September 2005. Although not as powerful as many hurricanes, Stan was part of a wider storm centre that caused widespread floods.

... ON THE SCENE ... ON THE SCENE ... ON THE SCENE ...

Tsunami teamwork

In December 2004 an undersea earthquake near Sumatra, Indonesia, created a massive tsunami which swept over the coasts of Indonesia, Sri Lanka, India and Thailand. Ian Woolverton, of the Australian Red Cross, travelled to the coastal village of Meulaboh, Indonesia, in January 2005. By then it was becoming clear that up to 40,000 people had died along this coast of the island of Sumatra.

Even in the first days after the disaster, Woolverton found Red Cross teams from Indonesia and other countries on the scene providing relief. 'At the hospital, the Japanese unloaded their three basic health kits. Each of the pre-packed kits comes in a large grey plastic box rather like a sturdy suitcase. Each can treat 10,000 people for up to three months.

'Clean water is a problem in the town. A team of Red Cross water and sanitation engineers from Spain are tackling this problem. They have already started supplying over 5,000 people per day with enough water to cook, clean and drink, but it is not enough. In the coming days more Red Cross workers are scheduled to arrive, increasing their capacity to supply water to 60,000 people per day.'

The overall Red Cross response was so successful that there was some money left over after the main recovery had been completed – and after representatives of other international organizations had left Central America. IFRC personnel remained in the region, where they continue to help local people adjust and rebuild their lives.

www.cruzroja.org.gt

WHAT DO YOU THINK?

One organization too many?

The International Red Cross does an excellent job in bringing relief to areas hit by disaster. But it is just one of many organizations that aim to provide relief. Do you think disaster victims would benefit if there were a single relief organization – rather than many different ones? Would having a single body make things happen more smoothly or would it be too big to control?

Working with others

No single group or organization – no
matter how skilled or experienced – can deal with all
the world's problems. In most countries facing a crisis,
international organizations work with national
governments and each other to provide the best help
in the fastest time. The Red Cross movement has a
long history of cooperating – in war zones, disaster
areas and where people are neediest.

*Red Cross and Red Crescent
workers team up with the
police to offer aid to remote
villages in Pakistan, after the
severe earthquake in 2005.*

This cooperation can take many forms. The ICRC and federation often work with each other, especially in places where military conflict is combined with serious natural problems and disasters. Both of these Red Cross branches, in turn, call on national societies for the latest information about where help is needed most.

One of many

In some of the most dramatic disasters, the Red Cross is just one of many international organizations to play a part. Its local knowledge – gained from its many national societies – enables it to guide other specialist organizations to their targets, and so make their efforts more effective.

One of the most dramatic examples of this cooperation came after the December 2004 Indian Ocean tsunami. Within a week, the world community had set aside more than £3.5 billion. Much of this money was spread between more than 30 international relief organizations (including the International Red Cross Movement).

Red Cross and Red Crescent teams sort out emergency supplies and set them aside, family by family, in the weeks following Pakistan's earthquake in October 2005.

Hunger in West Africa

The West African country of Niger faced a serious food shortage in the middle of 2005. Hunger was the main problem and the size and desert landscape of Niger made it hard to reach those who needed food most. The Federation of Red Cross and Red Crescent Societies led a coordinated international response.

The Red Cross Federation began by distributing enriched flour to hungry children in the worst-hit provinces. Then it used its links with the Niger Red Cross to find the best way to reach other parts of the country. That is where the World Food Programme (WFP) came in, using local Red Cross information to set up distribution bases in four towns. From these centres, the WFP sent food supplies to families throughout Niger.

The federation called on experts from other national societies to help. The British Red Cross, sent an emergency response unit (see page 26) which took medical and food experts to the problem areas.

The Norwegian Red Cross supplied 20 trucks to transport food and medicine throughout Niger. Other international groups, such as UNICEF and Medecins Sans Frontieres (a French-based medical organization), contributed to a committed team effort.

Villagers in Niger patiently wait for Red Cross emergency food supplies during the food crisis of 2005.

Closer to home

At its core, the International Red Cross movement is a network of national societies. These societies can advise the ICRC if their country faces military conflict, or the IFRC if it has been struck by a natural disaster. National societies also send representatives, teams, experts and equipment to help in other parts of the world.

Many people first learn of the Red Cross through the activities of the national societies in their own country in peacetime. Organizing blood drives and first-aid courses, visiting the sick and the elderly, providing health care for asylum seekers, distributing food to the needy – all these come under the Red Cross umbrella. The same humanitarian impulses that send Red Cross teams to war zones and earthquake sites operate closer to home

The tree of wishes

The people of eastern Europe have suffered great hardship in the past 70 years. First, their countries were overrun by the fighting of the Second World War. Then for nearly 50 years after the war ended in 1945, those countries came under the control of the Soviet Union. They lost most of their independence. Even now, 15 years after regaining independence, eastern European nations face hardship as they struggle to develop.

Belarus is one of the hardest-hit of these countries, yet its Red Cross national society constantly finds ways to improve life there and to raise people's spirits. Like many other Christians in eastern Europe, the people of Belarus celebrate Christmas in January. Christmas 2007 brought some wonderful surprises to the neediest children in Belarus. Volunteers from Belarus Red Cross Youth had a simple plan to translate Christmas spirit into reality for some of those children.

The plan was called the tree of wishes. Volunteers targetted shopping centres in six cities: Baranovichi, Brest, Grodno, Kamenets, Lida and Mogilev. In each shopping centre they set up a huge Christmas tree decorated with photographs of needy children: the poor, the sick, the handicapped, the abandoned. These children wrote their Christmas wishes on the back of the photographs. 'We were surprised at how modest the kids' wishes were,' said Vladimir, one of the volunteers. 'They asked Santa for sweets, for oranges and books. But most importantly, every child wanted to meet Santa.'

Meanwhile, volunteers approached shoppers and encouraged them to contribute towards the tree of wishes. The shoppers of Belarus – many of whom are badly-off themselves – proved to be very generous. The volunteers gathered the donated presents and bought more with money that had been given. Then they decided to take go a step further, by dressing as Santa when they distributed the presents to the children in hospitals, children's homes and orphanages. In the end, the volunteers distributed 2538 presents and more than 250 kg of sweets to 878 children.

New ways to raise funds

These include online donations, reducing tax for people who give to the Red Cross, donating goods to Red Cross charity shops and many other methods. Just like individuals and families, the International Red Cross needs to pay for all its activities. It relies on generous donations from governments and some large businesses (see pages 12–15), but millions of pounds still need to be raised. Most of this work is done by the national societies.

The British Red Cross is one of the most successful national societies in its fund-raising. Like other fund-raising organizations, the Red Cross has ways of making donations go further. People can sign documents which reduce the tax the Red Cross pays on donations. Or they can celebrate a wedding by asking guests to make donations to the Red Cross. Other people leave money to the Red Cross in their wills. In every case, the wider world benefits.

Bosnian Muslims, made homeless by the massacre in the city of Srebrenica, turned to the Red Cross for safety during 1995. The national committee of the Bosnian Red Cross continues to look after some of the Srebrenica refugees.

'The Life. Live it' kits are full of informative materials to help young people learn more about first aid.

Learning to save lives

The British Red Cross has an eye-catching way of teaching first aid and other safety issues to young people. Its teaching kit for young people aged between 11 and 14 is called 'The Life. Live it'. It makes teaching and learning first aid interesting and fun for schools and youth groups.

As well as containing traditional first aid teaching equipment such as bandages, dressings and a dummy (for resusitation techniques), the kit has a CD-rom with interactive quizzes, computer presentations and film footage. The Red Cross succeeds in doing more than merely entertaining young people with this kit.

Learning how to give first aid means that young people can save lives in all sorts of crises. They learn how to treat bleeding and shock; choking; injuries caused by road traffic accidents and other injuries and illnesses.

Looking to the future

Like any other large organization, the Red Cross needs to adapt to a changing world in order to continue to fulfil its mission worldwide. It is nearing the end of Strategy 2010, the ten-year IFRC plan adopted in October 1999.

Moving on from that, the Red Cross movement as a whole will be looking at its strengths and weaknesses in order to successfully face the future.

Red Cross HIV/AIDS teaching sessions target some of the youngest people in southern Africa, a region of the world where the disease has spread most widely.

Gathering of youth

'The future of the Red Cross is in the hands of young people,' said Ullah Nuchrawaty Usman, an Indonesian Red Cross board member. 'We want them to understand the humanitarian values of the organization and realize the difference they can make, especially to the lives of people in distress.'

Usman organizes the Jumbara (an Indonesian Red Cross national youth camp) which promotes both the national society and the wider movement. The Jumbara is held every five years and the latest was in July 2006. Indonesians understand the importance of the Red Cross after experiencing two major natural disasters – the 2004 tsunami and the 2005 earthquake. The first-hand experience of young Indonesians who benefitted from Red Cross assistance will draw in more young people to become future leaders.

More than 3000 young people attended the 2006 Jumbara. This included those from Indonesia as well as 42 guests from the Red Cross and Red Crescent Societies of Brunei,

China, Germany, Hong Kong, Japan, Korea, Malaysia, Myanmar, Netherlands and Singapore. The message does seem to be filtering from one nation to another. As Bjorn, a German delegate, observed: 'We are overwhelmed by what the Red Cross, especially the Indonesian Red Cross, is doing to help the tsunami survivors. We want to be a part of it, even in a small way.'

A young volunteer helps keep the pot boiling at mealtime during the Red Cross Jumbara (youth camp) held in Indonesia in July 2006.

Imagine trying to make these predictions ten years ago. In the late 1990s, many felt that the world was more peaceful. The Second World War had ended more than 50 years before, and the rivalry between the US and the Soviet Union – the cold war – was over.

However, terrorism has become a constant concern. Also many people believe that we are raising the Earth's temperature by releasing more gases into the atmosphere. This rise in temperature might lead to more – and fiercer – storms and other natural disasters. The wider Red Cross movement must recognize this changing world.

Finding new partnerships

Just like many national governments, international organizations such as the Red Cross have begun teaming up with private companies. Why? One major reason is that big companies have lots of money, some of which can be shared to spread the Red Cross message. An association with the Red Cross can enhance the image of a company, by sending a message that it does not just operate to make a profit, but also recognizes that it has a responsibility to society. The Red Cross, for its part, can help a joint project earn the public's respect.

The British Red Cross has set up a partnership with the Japanese car-maker Toyota. In May 2005, it launched a three-year 'Don't be a Bystander' campaign. This programme is aimed at both parents and children, teaching them about first aid and road safety. The campaign came about because the British Red Cross and Toyota had conducted a survey in Britain, to see how much young people knew about first aid and safety issues. The survey showed that 60 per cent of children aged between nine and thirteen (those most at risk from road traffic accidents) lacked the knowledge of first aid to help themselves or others at the scene of an accident.

'Don't be a Bystander' ran 150 first-aid sessions all round the country over three years, in venues such as shopping centres, theme parks, schools, town centres and even beaches. The goal of the campaign is to teach 100,000 people some essential first aid skills.

Hospital handover

The International Red Cross movement must always look for ways to save money, like any international organization concerned about its future. Savings in one area can be passed on to help needier people. One way to achieve this aim is to hand over responsibility for some Red Cross activities to local people. The local population acquires vital skills – and sometimes equipment – while the Red Cross can move staff and supplies elsewhere.

Lopiding Hospital in northern Kenya is a good example of such a partnership. On 30 June 2006, the ICRC handed control of the hospital over to the Kenyan authorities. Lopiding began in 1987 as an ICRC field hospital, treating people who had been wounded in the civil war in neighbouring Sudan. With 700 beds, it was the largest field hospital in the world at its peak. In 19 years as a Red Cross hospital, it treated 60,000 people.

At Lopiding more than 4300 people received artificial limbs. Hospital doctors carried out about 4000 operations a year when fighting was at its worst. More than 300 Sudanese medical workers were trained at the hospital, returning to help patients in their own country. Their training is a legacy of the International Red Cross Movement. But so is the hospital, with its two operating theatres, special intensive care unit, medical lab and pharmacy. The people in northern Kenya have gained long-term benefits from the presence of the Red Cross in their midst.

At its core, as ever, are the national societies. Whatever direction the movement takes, the national societies must remain true to the four core areas that make the Red Cross special.
• Promotion of humanitarian values and principles
• Disaster response
• Disaster preparations
• Health and care in the community
In the next decade the Red Cross will celebrate its 150th birthday. Combining the core values with new approaches will give the movement – and the world as a whole – a lasting present.

*Opposite page
Red Cross medical staff remained at Lopiding Hospital throughout the transition period until Kenyans could replace them in 2006.*

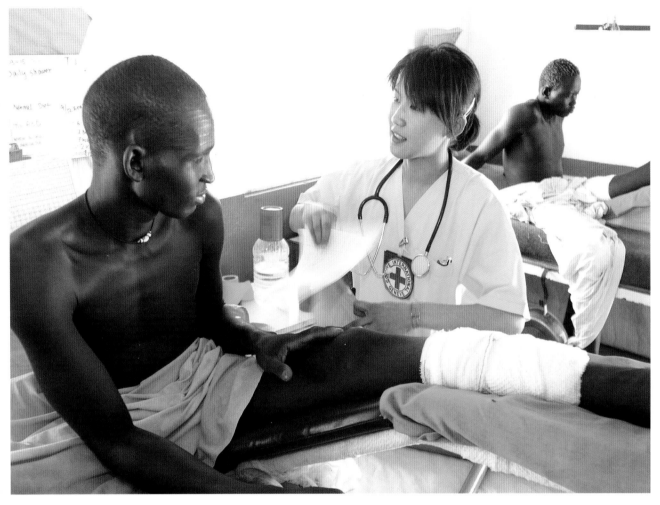

What changes would you make?

Imagine it was your job to look hard at the International Red Cross movement and to make changes. What would you do? Would you aim for a greater emphasis on national societies, so that relief efforts can be streamlined from above more quickly? Should the Red Cross deal with education and long-term health improvement, rather than responding rapidly to crises? Should it drop any religious references (cross, crescent) from its emblem?

WHAT DO YOU THINK?

How you can help

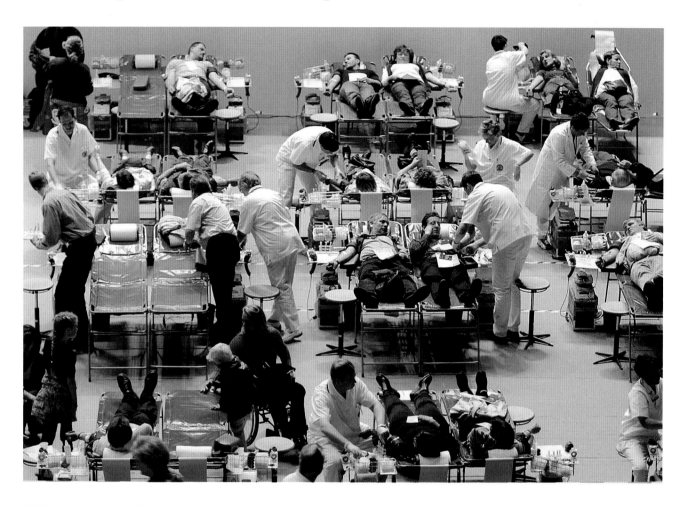

The Red Cross movement relies on its national societies, which makes it easy for young people to take part in its activities. The societies break down further into regional branches (eg south east in the UK, or New South Wales in Australia) and city branches.

At every level, people – including young people – are encouraged to take part in activities. Red Cross volunteers are the backbone of the movement, and they help more than just the Red Cross. Many people who are now helping to shape the world – political leaders, education specialists, doctors and nurses – have been involved with the Red Cross throughout their lives.

The Red Cross believes that people are getting the message about many of the aims of the Red Cross aims. In the past ten years more and more people have donated blood at sessions like this one in Dortmund, Germany.

The gift of life

The emblem of the Red Cross calls to mind not only the Swiss flag but also the blood on the battlefield that affected Henry Dunant so deeply. Blood remains an important part of the Red Cross – particularly in the way the movement collects it from healthy people. Red Cross national societies have been involved in blood-donating sessions for decades. Donated blood is held in laboratories called blood banks. It is used to help people who have lost blood through serious injury or during operations. Most Red Cross societies have a minimum age for donating blood (in the UK it is 17), but younger people can encourage their parents and older relatives to take part.

Healthy breakfasts

Some of the most important Red Cross projects aim to promote healthy living. The Good Start Breakfast Club is an Australian Red Cross programme which does just that. Young volunteers join the project to help educate people – especially children – about good nutrition. Children can eat a hearty breakfast in the familiar setting of their school. Why breakfast? And why in a rich country like Australia? Many medical experts consider breakfast to be the most important meal of the day. Going without breakfast is bad for us physically (because we lose essential foods) but also psychologically (children find it harder to concentrate at school if they don't eat breakfast). Between 5 and 30 per cent of young Australians miss breakfast. The problem is worse among poorer people. The Good Start Breakfast Club is a step towards giving everyone a better chance every day – and in life generally.

WHAT DO YOU THINK?

What else could young people do?

Can you think of any other ways to help young people play a bigger role in the Red Cross? Does your school or youth group have a connection with the Red Cross? If not, could you set one up and make a lasting difference?

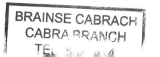

Glossary

allies Individuals or countries that work together in a struggle. In the Second World War, the term referred to the countries (led by France, China, the United Kingdom, the United States and the Soviet Union) which opposed Germany, Japan and their partners.

asylum seeker A person escaping danger, violence or hunger in his or her own country.

civilian Someone who is not part of an armed force such as an army, navy or air force.

colony A region of the world controlled or governed by an outside country.

communist Someone who believes in a system in which all property is owned by the community and each person contributes and receives according to their ability and needs. A communist government provides work, health care, education and housing, but may deny people certain freedoms.

convert To convince someone or a group of people to change their religious beliefs.

Crimean War A war fought from 1854-6 in which Russia fought Great Britain, France and Turkey.

drought A prolonged lack of rain, which can lead to food crops dying in the fields.

emblem A sign or design that acts as the symbol of a group or an organization.

First World War A war fought mainly in Europe between 1914 and 1918.

Herculean Involving enormous effort, which was required of the Greek hero Hercules.

humanely With care and consideration for other human beings and animals.

humanitarian Helping to improve the happiness or living conditions of people.

impartiality Willingness to see both sides of an argument.

muster To gather or assemble a group.

neutrality The aim of not taking sides in an argument or in an armed conflict.

news media Newspapers, radio, television and the Internet as ways of passing on news.

personnel The people who work for or on behalf of an organization.

revenge Punishment designed to retaliate against someone or something.

Richter Scale A scale for measuring the strength of earthquakes. A reading of five or more indicates a destructive earthquake.

sanctuary Protection from arrest or attack.

Second World War A war waged around the world, in which the Allies fought against Germany, Japan and their partners.

shock A reaction which causes many of the body's functions to shut down as a result of severe injury or illness.

Soviet Union The name given to a country that included Russia and 14 of its neighbours, which united to form a larger communist country from 1917 to 1991.

torture To hurt someone in order to get information from them, or to force them to confess to something.

tsunami A high, fast-moving wave produced when there is an earthquake under the ocean.

UNICEF The United Nations Children's Fund, an international organization devoted to the world's children.

universality Having the same values around the world and not favouring one group over another.

voluntary Choosing to do something and not being forced to do so.

Further reading

The Red Cross Movement (*World Watch* series) J Bingham (Raintree, 2004)

Red Cross (Humanitarian Organizations) A Parry (Chelsea House, 2005)

International Red Cross (World Organizations) K Prior and R Perkins (Franklin Watts, 2001)

The British Red Cross (Taking Action!) L Spilsbury (Heinemann Library, 2001)

Websites

www.redcross.org.uk/
The home page of the British Red Cross with information aimed at young people.

www.redcross.org.au/
The Australian site with news of Red Cross activities around the country and other links.

http://www.redcross.org.uk/firstaid
Details of the first aid partnership between the British Red Cross and Toyota.

http://www.takingitglobal.org/
Links up young people to find new ways of making positive changes around the world.

http://www.ifrc.org/youth
The young people's section of the IFRC website with quizzes, news stories, activities, etc.

Index

ambulances 18
artificial limbs 40
asylum seekers 33

blankets 6
blood donation 33, 42, 43
bombs 18, 20

charity shops 35
civil war 6, 12, 19, 40
civilians 9, 19, 22
cold war 39
Crimean War 8, 9

development 16, 17, 34
donations 15, 34, 35
droughts 26
Dunant, Henry 9, 10, 11, 43

earthquakes 24, 25, 26, 28, 30,
   31, 33, 38
emergencies 7, 26, 32
European Union 15

first aid 33, 36, 39
First World War 13
food 24, 27, 32, 33
floods 28
fund raising 15, 35

Geneva Convention 13, 19

health 17, 41, 43
HIV/AIDS 37
hospitals 18, 19, 24, 28, 34, 40
hurricanes 26, 27, 28

international humanitarian law
   (IHL) 19, 21

landslides 28

medical aid 7, 18, 19, 25

natural disasters 7, 17, 26, 31,
   33, 39
Nightingale, Florence 8, 9
Nobel Peace Prize 10

prisoners of war 12, 18, 19

Red Crescent 7, 14, 15, 16, 17,
   21, 22, 31, 32
Red Cross movement
   core values 7
   Don't be a Bystander campaign
      39
   emblem 9, 21, 43
   emergency response units 26,
      32
   inspectors 21
   international committee
      (ICRC) 9, 14, 15, 16, 17, 18,
      19, 20, 23, 26, 31, 33

international conferences 16
international federation 15
   name 16
   national societies 7, 14, 15, 17,
      22, 26, 28, 31, 32, 33, 35, 40,
      41, 42, 43
   structure 16, 17
   symbols 14
Red Crystal 14, 21
refugees 35

Second World War 18, 34, 39
shelter 13, 24, 27
soldiers 8, 9, 11, 13
Solferino, Battle of 11
storms 26, 28, 39

terrorism 23, 39
tsunamis 28, 31, 38

United Nations 15, 20

volunteers 11, 18, 22, 25, 27, 34,
   38, 42, 43

warfare 7, 12, 16, 17, 18, 20
water 24, 28
weapons 13, 22
World Food Programme 32

youth camps 38